I Say a Little Prayer for You

To Aaliyah and Marie

ISBN 0-439-45616-9

12 11 10 9 8 7 6 5 4 3 2   2 3 4 5 6 7/0

Printed in the U.S.A.   09

First Scholastic paperback printing, September 2002

Designed by Mandy Sherlicker

I Say a Little Prayer for You

Adapted from the original song by Burt Bacharach and Hal David

Illustrated by Karin Littlewood

SCHOLASTIC INC.

New York Toronto London Auckland Sydney
Mexico City New Delhi Hong Kong Buenos Aires

The moment I wake up,
before I put on my make up...

I say a little prayer for you.

While combing my hair now,

and wondering what dress to wear now...

I say a little
prayer for you.

Forever, forever you'll
stay in my heart,
and I will love you.
Forever and ever
we never will part.
Oh, how I'll love you.

Together, together, that's
how it must be.

To live without you
would only mean heartbreak for me.

I run for the bus, dear.
While riding I think of us, dear...
I say a little prayer for you.

At work I just take time,
and all through my coffee break time...
I say a little prayer for you.

HAPPY BIRTHDAY
HAPPY
THDAY
PPY
DAY

Forever, forever you'll stay in my heart,
and I will love you.

Forever and ever we never will part.
Oh, how I'll love you.

HAPPY BIRTHDAY

Together, together,
that's how it must be.
To live without you
would only mean
heartbreak for me.

I say a little
prayer for you.

APPY
THDAY

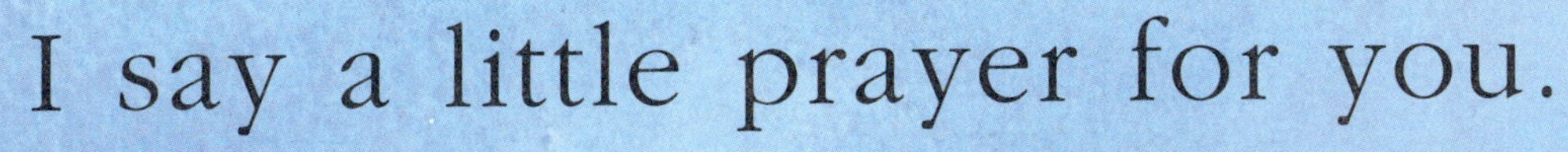

I say a little prayer for you.

Forever, forever you'll stay in my heart,

and I will love you.

Forever and ever we never will part.

Oh, how I'll love you.

Together, together,
that's how it must be.

To live without you
would only mean heartbreak for me.

HAPPY
BIRTH
BIRTH
HAPPY
BIRTH

Answer my prayer.
You know every day
I say a little prayer.

I say a little prayer for you.

THE REASON SHE HAS SPARKLES

By
Melody Goliday

Illustrated By
Antonella Cammarano

The Reason She Has Sparkles
Copyright © 2021

Author: Melody Goliday
Illustator: Antonella Cammarno

ISBN: 978-1-647753-22-1

Dedicated to:

My daughter Ariane M. loving you is easy. I pray that you wake up everyday, loving yourself, choosing yourself and knowing your worth. It was not until I became your mother that I knew a life of unconditional love. From that moment, I knew I had to love myself a little more in order to love you much more.

I want you to always love yourself with no limits, believe in yourself and never negotiate your happiness or the love you have for yourself. Be all that you can be and never stop dreaming.

I will always love you!

–Mommy

Pretty brown girl, the moment you opened your eyes, you were given a sparkle that could not be deprived.

Cherish that sparkle with all your pride. For that same sparkle will join you in life on that ride.

Your sparkle will grow, and you will see many traits
that makes you different from me – pretty brown
girl with your warm personality.

Your sparkles are different and that is the reality,
but that doesn't stop them from being sparkly.

Oh, pretty brown girl, it's nothing like being yourself. Never be afraid to ask for help.

If you ever feel lost and not like yourself, think of your sparkle, it always helps.

Pretty brown girl, although you were born with
a different sparkle, you will still shine.

Never dim your light to fit in line. When you wake
up each morning, choose to be one of a kind.

Pretty brown girl, you are enough! Your kinky hair, the clothes you wear and even that smile that is always there.

Other people's sparkle
could not dare compare.

You do not need more to fill any void. And
you may not always have your favorite toy.

But never let anyone steal your joy. For
the sparkle in you cannot be destroyed.

You will not always have good days. And you
are still learning all your unique ways.

Be gentle with yourself on your bad days.
That sparkle in you will not fade.

It's okay to get upset, pretty brown girl count to three and reset. Love yourself a little more; you can take a deep breath or even count to four.

Acknowledge what you are feeling; it can not be ignored. Remember your sparkle as a reward.

Today is a new day pretty brown girl let's try again, dust yourself off; it's time to win.

We have made plans to be great; let the sparkle begin. Greatness truly starts within.

Believe in yourself pretty brown girl; it will take you far. No more wishing upon a star.

Let's set those goals and raise the bar. Your sparkle is with you, near or far.

The moment you think that you should not
believe, those goals you set will not achieve.

You will start to feel like some tumbleweed.
But your sparkle will never ever leave.

Pretty brown girl, you have potential. To get whatever it is that you have wished for.

Be dedicated and stay focus. For that sparkle in you does not go unnoticed.

Pretty brown girl, you can do it! As long as
you always put your mind to it.

There will be times when you will start to feel discouraged.
The sparkle in you will always encourage.

Pretty brown girl, you are the motivation. Girls like you deserve a standing ovation, in this world full of temptation.

Your sparkle shines bright like the lights on a spaceship.

Pretty brown girl, keep your head high
because crowns should never fall.

Always have confidence in yourself and
stand tall. You were born with a sparkle
that will never be dull.

To all the pretty brown girls around the world. Know that no matter what anyone else says, you are beautiful.

You are enough with just being you. Love yourself so much that your sparkle will always shine.

Getting to know the author

MELODY GOLIDAY,

I am a mother of a sweet little girl. Writing has always been a way for me to express myself. In my spare time, I journal; it helps me feel free in a world of chaos.

My passion for self-love has grown over the years, and my goal is to instill that in the youth through reading.

In my experience, it becomes very challenging to learn the language of self-love as you get older and try to live in a world of many things.

Made in the USA
Columbia, SC
26 March 2021